Stepping Through History

SHOPS AND MARKETS

PEGGY BURNS

Wayland

Stepping Through History

Money
News
The Post
Shops and Markets
Travel
Writing

Editor: Vanessa Cummins
Series designer: John Christopher

First published in 1995 by Wayland (Publishers) Limited
61 Western Road, Hove, East Sussex BN3 1JD, England

British Library Cataloguing in Publication Data
Burns, Peggy
Shops and Markets. – (Stepping Through History series)
I. Title II. Series
381.109

ISBN 0 7502 1521 6

Picture Acknowledgements
The Publishers would like to thank the following for allowing their pictures to be used in this book: AKG 8 (below), 11, 12, timeline (middle); Bridgeman Art Library 4 (below); Birdseye Walls plc 23; Chapel Studios 29 (above); E.T. Archive **cover (top)**; Marks and Spencers plc 19 (above); Mary Evans 10, 18, 20 (above); Eye Ubiquitous **cover (left)** (Tim Page), **title page** (Frank Spooner), 12 (Dave Forbister), 15 (Mike Southern), 17 below (Frank Leather); Robert Harding **cover (right)**, spine, 16 (main), 24, timeline (bottom); Michael Holford 4 (above), 21 (above); Panos 17 (above), 25; Photri 9 (below), 14, 21 (below), 26, 27, 29 (below); Ann Ronan 13 (above), timeline (top); Frank Spooner 22 (below); Tony Stone **cover (main)**, 6, 7, 22, 28; Topham 5 (above), 7 (above); Woolworth Corporation (USA) 20 (below). The artwork on page 13 is by Barbara Loftus.

Typeset by Strong Silent Type
Printed and bound in Italy by G. Canale & C.S.p.A., Turin

CONTENTS

THE DAYS BEFORE SHOPS

Eight thousand years ago, there were no shops at all. Most people lived by fishing, hunting and gathering food from wild plants. There was no farming until 5000 BC.

Right: Farm tools made of copper and bronze used 3,700 years ago.

Around 5000 BC, people began to clear the ground to plant crops using simple tools. At first tools were made of stone and later of copper and other metals. *Flints* and metals, used for axe heads and digging tools, were carried hundreds of kilometres by traders.

Right: Clay jars for wine and olive oil were carried in the holds of ships like this.

Copper was taken by boat to Egypt from the surrounding countries. In return, the traders were given dates, wheat and animal-hides (used for leather and fur). This exchange of goods is called barter. Barter will only work if the people exchanging goods want what they are offered. Sometimes this means that goods have to be carried over long distances in order to barter and exchange them with other goods.

Left: The Egyptians were successful farmers and traded food for the tools they used for harvesting.

Ships from Africa and India carried many goods including gold, *ivory*, silk and pottery to towns and villages all over the **Middle East**. People began to trade with others in different parts of the world. Trade routes such as the silk roads were opened, joining Asia with western Europe.

Items that everyone wanted, such as small pieces of valuable metal, began to be exchanged for goods. Small thumbnail-sized shapes made from gold and silver were used as coins in the Middle East about 2,600 years ago. Although barter still took place, money in the form of coins, gradually took over.

BARTER AND MONEY

Barter is still used today. The Dani people of Papua New Guinea and Irian Jaya trade arrowheads, pigs' teeth and birds of paradise feathers in return for knives, axes and food. Pigs are very valuable too and are exchanged in the same way as money. For instance, when a bride gets married her family may give a dowry of pigs. The pigs are given to the parents of the groom in order to celebrate the marriage.

This Dani man is wearing a wig made of human hair, decorated with daisies, grasses and feathers.

THE FIRST MARKETS AND SHOPS

Early farmers sometimes produced more food than they needed and wanted to exchange their extra crops and livestock. Similarly, *craftspeople* who had made pots or other goods wanted to exchange them for food. The first markets began when these people started meeting together to barter or to buy each other's goods and produce.

A Roman tablet showing a customer sitting down ready to be served in a shop.

The forum in Rome, Italy, as it is today. Can you imagine how it looked in the past?

The Romans built many towns throughout their empire. At the centre of each town was usually an open space, called a forum. These market places were used to sell many goods and farm produce. There were small buildings where craftspeople worked, selling the goods they made at the front of their workshops. This is where the word 'shop' comes from. At its height, the Roman Empire was very well organized, trade grew quickly and shops sprang up in many towns.

Today, we know exactly what Roman shops were like by studying *archaeological sites*. In AD 79, the volcano Vesuvius erupted. A deep layer of ash buried the town of Pompeii, near the modern city of Naples in Italy. The town was dug out from the ash in the nineteenth century, and it looked as if the streets, houses, shops, and even people had been frozen in time.

A Roman wall painting found in Pompeii. It shows a baker selling bread from a street stall, just like fast food is sold today.

Pompeii had a forum where traders had stalls and there was a covered fish market. Many streets had shops of one kind or another. There were even fast-food shops where customers could buy takeaway food. After the Roman Empire ended in the fifth century less trade took place.

Trade in Europe and Asia began to grow again around AD 1100. People moved from the countryside to find work in towns. In the towns, people needed food and clothing which they could not produce themselves. Shops became more important and market places became the centre of town life.

A paved street in Pompeii. This street was wide enough to allow two chariots to pass each other in opposite directions.

Market places were also important to Chinese town-life. Marco Polo, an Italian merchant, travelled to China in the thirteenth century and wrote in great detail about life there. He described the large city of Hangchow as having hundreds of shops as well as fifteen different market places.

Right: A modern wall painting of the Aztec market in the ancient city of Tenochtitlan.

AN AZTEC MARKET

By the fourteenth century, the *Aztecs* had built a huge central market close to their capital city, Tenochtitlan (now modern-day Mexico City). The Spanish conquistadors who invaded the city were astonished when they saw this market. One soldier said it was better run than any he had seen in Europe. People had to carry everything to the market because the Aztecs had no wheeled carts. Cocoa beans, *jade*, rubber, feathers and other goods were sold in the market. There were rules for buying and selling with a judge present to settle arguments.

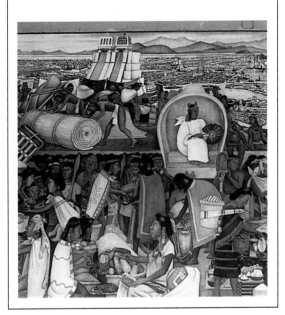

PEDLARS, MARKETS AND GUILDS

Village people often relied on travelling sellers known as pedlars to buy goods. Pedlars carried small items, such as brushes, ribbons and pots and pans.

In Japan, wandering craftspeople travelled around the country. They included woodworkers who made dishes of wood using simple *lathes* which they carried with them.

A pedlar and his customers at a fair in Scotland in the early nineteenth century.

As well as regular markets, the custom grew up of having larger markets, called fairs, with entertainments as well as goods for sale. As early as the ninth century, Chinese officials controlled what took place at many fairs. Boxing, strongmen, juggling, fire-eating and other street entertainments were allowed on certain days.

By the twelfth century, shopping was also popular in China. Kaifeng city (800 kilometres to the north-west of Shanghai) had stalls serving tea and food and an arched bridge lined on either side with shops.

Above: A busy scene at a cloth market in The Netherlands in the sixteenth century.

Right: Today, Chinese hawkers still sell their goods from blankets laid on the ground.

Hawkers, who travelled around selling goods, showed customers their wares laid out on blankets or low tables. The shoppers were entertained by street entertainers with performing monkeys or by going to see a fortune teller.

At the same time, fairs became popular in Europe. One of the largest fairs was held at Novgorod in Russia. European fairs were often held on religious holidays and festival days and attracted merchants from far and wide.

GUILDS

Craftspeople using the same materials, or making similar goods, had many common interests. They often lived in the same areas of the town, and used the same skills and tools. Because of this, they formed into groups, called *guilds*.

There were guilds in Egypt and China over four thousand years ago. Guilds of *merchants* were formed in Europe in the eleventh century. Later, guilds of craftspeople were formed. Guilds often had their own special god or saint to protect them. Guilds were powerful, setting standards of work and prices, protecting the interests of their members and giving money to the poor to build schools. In China, governments even used the guilds to collect *taxes* and help run the cities.

Tradesmen in Paris in the sixteenth century had their own guilds.

LUXURY GOODS

Shopping became increasingly popular in the eighteenth and nineteenth centuries and there were many more things to buy in the shops. Wealthy people enjoyed shopping for new goods and the latest fashions, and some city shops became well-known for the *quality* of their goods and the service they gave their customers.

Right: A mother and child choosing sweets in a luxury sweet shop in England in 1821.

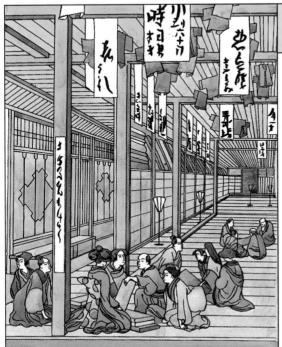

MITSUI DRAPERY

Wealthy people in Japan visited the Mitsui *drapery shop* in Edo (now called Tokyo). Lengths of silk were imported from China and the store had a money exchange where money was lent to merchants. By 1700, the shop had a staff of 130 workers and could make material into clothing while the customer waited drinking cups of tea.

A modern picture of Japanese ladies wearing kimonos and choosing cloth at the Mitsui drapery.

Skilled craftspeople in seventeenth-century Williamsburg made luxury goods such as musical instruments. This photograph shows the Williamsburg museum, which has restored the musical instrument workshop to how it was in 1750.

In the eighteenth century, goods such as tea, sugar, pineapples and oranges were introduced to Europe for the first time. Fine *porcelain* and furniture from China were sold there too. All these goods were much admired and could only be afforded by very rich people.

By 1750, in the town built by settlers at Williamsburg, Virginia, in North America, the shops were full of goods from Europe with some items from as far away as China and India. Dutch traders, in the islands we now call Indonesia, bought *spices* for the shops of Europe and the Middle East. Spices were also sent to the settlers in North America and other parts of the world.

By the 1760s, highly-skilled workers had set up workshops, especially in New England in North America, making silver goods, clocks, musical instruments and fine furniture. In Japan, luxury goods included Chinese silk and soap, which had to be *imported*.

SHOP DESIGN

In some parts of the world, shops have changed little in the last 500 years. In Old Delhi, India and the Grand *Bazaar* in Istanbul, Turkey, the shops are small and are often the home of shopkeepers as well.

The shop fronts have no glass and wooden shutters are used to close the shop at night. Goods are often made at the back of the shop and sold at the front. In the Grand Bazaar, the narrow streets are roofed over to keep them cool and protect the goods from the hot sun.

In the seventeenth and eighteenth centuries, shops in the towns and cities of Europe began to use panes of glass in windows overlooking the street. Glass was cheaper than it had been and gave protection against bad weather. Customers were served at counters inside the shop.

Shopping undercover at the Grand Bazaar in Istanbul, Turkey. Why do you think it is so dark?

An eighteenth-century French shop front made of wood. The windows contain small panes of glass.

In the nineteenth century, larger panes of glass, and then **plate glass**, made displays in the windows an important way of advertising. The new glass was expensive and only the larger shops could afford it. However, displaying goods in the windows brought in more customers and sales increased.

Window displays were made more attractive by the use of lighting. The larger shops introduced gas lighting for the first time in the 1850s and electrical lighting in the 1880s. Electricity also made it possible to build lifts and **escalators** by the end of the century. Advertising in newspapers and magazines became popular after about 1880 when better machinery and supplies of paper made daily newspapers cheap and plentiful.

Shopkeepers hung signs outside their shops to advertize what they sold. A dairy often showed a painted sign of a cow. Japanese shops used a curtain made of dark blue cloth which was hung at the door of the shop. The cloth had a design in the middle which was the trademark of the shop. Writing was added to describe what was sold there. When the shop was closed the curtain was taken down.

Above: Walking under these over-hanging shop fronts in Singapore keeps shoppers cool and dry.

In the cities of India and south-east Asia, wide tree-lined streets with rows of shops built by the end of the nineteenth century. The shops were built out over the pavement on columns so that customers could walk in the cool, avoiding the hot sunshine. Shopping was becoming more international as European stores were opened in Singapore, Bombay, and other Eastern cities.

Shop signs can be seen in many streets today. These are in Salzburg, Austria.

THE FIRST DEPARTMENT STORES

Great changes in the ways that goods were made began to take place in the eighteenth and nineteenth centuries. The number and type of goods produced were greatly increased by the discovery that steam could provide power to drive machinery.

New types of machinery were invented and new materials were used. The first railways were built in the nineteenth century. Trains carried goods quickly and cheaply from place to place and helped shopkeepers receive and deliver goods. Shoppers could also reach towns more easily.

A French couple, Monsieur and Madame Boucicault, had the idea of opening a large store which would sell many different goods in separate departments under one roof.

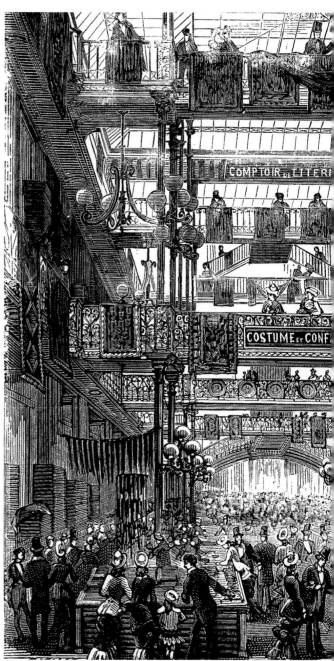

Right: The new Marks and Spencer opened in Paris in 1994.

In 1852, they opened the world's first department store, Bon Marché, in Paris. The idea quickly caught on and department stores were opened in other large cities such as London, New York and Moscow. People looked with wonder at the richness and size of these department stores and at the huge variety of goods which they sold. One cartoon showed a shop assistant asking a customer the way to the toy department because he was lost!

Chain stores selling a wide range of goods cheaply began to appear towards the end of the century. Marks and Spencer started as a market stall in Leeds, England, in 1884. Today, there are branches in many parts of the world.

Left: The Bon Marché department store opened in 1852.

WOOLWORTH FIVE AND DIME

Frank Woolworth, who started up the chain store Woolworth, was born on a farm in New York State, USA in 1852. While he was working in a village shop he heard of a store having a counter selling only five-cent goods. He thought this was a good idea and started a five-cent store in a nearby town but the business failed. In 1879, he built another store in Pennsylvania. The store was successful and he added items costing a dime, or ten cents. Other members of his family were brought in to help and more stores were opened.

The first Woolworth store opened in Lancaster, Pennsylvania, USA in 1879.

Woolworth began buying goods which had been specially made for his stores. In 1911, he built a famous tower block called the Woolworth Building in New York. At that time the tower block was the tallest building in the world. When he died in 1919, there were more than one thousand Woolworth stores around the world.

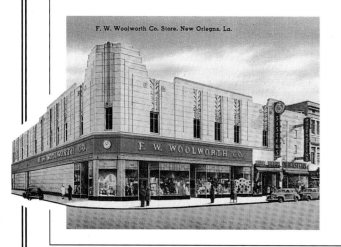

A Woolworth store in New Orleans built in the 1930s.

PACKAGING AND PRESERVING

Food has been dried, *preserved* and packaged since earliest times. In cold climates fish and other food could be kept frozen. In warm climates grapes and tomatoes could be sun dried.

Glass jars and cans made of tin plate were used between 1800 and 1850 but the food sometimes went bad. Australia started canning meat and sending it to Britain in 1847 and canning meat on a large scale started in Chicago in 1868. By 1900, new methods of canning food made certain that it did not go bad.

Hand-made glass was one of the earliest types of packaging. This blue glass bottle was used by the Romans 2,000 years ago.

Before 1850, packaging was mainly limited to wooden barrels, glass jars and boxes or *jute sacks*. Paper was expensive and was only made in sheets. Paper bags came into use when new machinery allowed paper to be made in large rolls. Shop keepers made bags from paper and weighed out the amount each customer wanted into separate bags.

Wine stored in oak barrels which help to improve its flavour. Barrels have been used since Egyptian times over 4,000 years ago.

By the 1870s, refrigerators were being used to carry food long distances by train. Ships with refrigeration units in their cargo holds carried meat from Uruguay, in South America, to France in 1877 and frozen lamb was sent to Britain from New Zealand in 1880.

Above: Refrigeration units on trains have revolutionized the way food is sent to shops and markets.

Crushed containers made of plastic, aluminium and tin waiting to be recycled. What do you think happens next?

The biggest growth in packaging materials has come about in the last forty years. A new process of coating card with wax has made paper packaging suitable for liquids such as milk. Plastic bags and containers, as well as aluminium cans, are light and strong. They have also helped shopkeepers to sell a wider range of goods. The amount of packaging has increased because supermarkets have goods packaged so that the customer can see what he or she is buying.

Many methods of preserving food have been developed in the last seventy years. Removing the water to make **dehydrated** soups and other food means they take up little space and last a long time. Vacuum packing and rapid deep freezing first appeared in the 1950s and now stores have large refrigerated cabinets where the food can be displayed.

Irradiation allows fresh produce, such as strawberries, to be preserved for many days. Irradiation exposes the fruit to radiation which kills bacteria, moulds and insects. The amount of radiation is very low and does not harm the person eating the fruit. However, in some countries, scientists are not certain how safe irradiation is and will not permit food to be treated in this way.

BIRDSEYE FROZEN FOODS

Clarence Birdseye was born in New York City in 1886. When he was twenty-two he went to college and studied science. Between 1912 and 1916, he went on a fur-trading expedition to Labrador in the far north of Canada. While he was there he noticed that many types of food would keep for a very long time when frozen.

Clarence Birdseye.

When he returned home he carried out experiments to find a method for freezing food on a large scale. In 1924, he helped form a company, later called Birdseye General Foods. In 1949, he invented a process which cut down the freezing time from eighteen to one and a half hours. He died in 1956, but the international company he had started is still going strong with frozen fish fingers as one of its biggest sellers.

BEHIND THE SCENES

Thirty years ago, trucks and ships were specially designed to carry refrigerated containers to transport food. Sometimes the air is replaced with *nitrogen* inside the containers in order to keep the food fresh. Container ships can now keep fruit and vegetables fresh for many days.

Sending goods on aeroplanes has become faster and cheaper in recent years and airports can handle cargoes much more quickly than in the past. As a result, peas grown in Zambia or Kenya can be bought in the supermarkets of Saudi Arabia and The Netherlands within two days of them being picked.

Containers being loaded on to a ship in the United Arab Emirates.

Peas can be grown and picked in Zambia, and sent to Europe to be sold in supermarkets.

Today's shopkeepers buy their goods from wholesalers who store goods bought from manufacturers abroad in large *warehouses*. Wholesale goods cost the shopkeepers far less than they sell them for. The price the wholesaler charges the shopkeeper is sometimes known as the retail price. The profit made by the shopkeeper is the difference between the retail price and the price charged to the customer.

Goods in this warehouse are bar coded and sent by computer to the correct loading bay.

Supermarkets and department stores sometimes own factories and sell their own **brands**. Also they buy cheaply in large amounts directly from farmers and factories where the goods are produced. As a result, they can often sell many goods more cheaply to the customer than individual shopkeepers can.

One problem that all traders have is knowing what the customer wants and needs. All shopkeepers with goods they cannot sell will lose money. Also a shopkeeper will lose a sale or make less profit if he or she has run out of goods the customer wants.

Modern supermarkets and department stores are solving this problem by using **information technology** (IT). All goods are coded with a bar-code and number which an **infra-red scanner** can read at the **check-out**. Details of the product obtained by the scanner are sent to a central computer and at the same time the information and price are printed on the customer's receipt. This information is then sent to the head office of the shop by means of a computer link. Stock can then be ordered when required, often from the other side of the world.

Cartons of Canadian salt cod-fish being carried by fork-lift truck in the warehouse.

SHOPPING – TODAY AND TOMORROW

In those parts of the world where many people are rich enough to own cars, out-of-town shopping centres are very popular. These centres may contain many different types of shops as well as cinemas and restaurants.

Nearby car parks make shopping very easy for people with cars. Large department stores and shopping centres provide many different services to help shoppers. They may have play areas for children, a shop assistant to help carry goods to the car park; ice-rinks, indoor gardens with waterfalls and huge screens showing the latest pop music videos.

A large, modern shopping centre in Toronto, Canada. A fountain and glass roof make it an attractive place to shop in.

Today, there is more choice in the way we shop than ever before. Mail-order *catalogues* have been in use for over a hundred years but buying goods from television shopping channels is quite recent. Home-computers can be linked to stores so that people can order goods from their computer screen. Already stores have customer-operated computers from which information about goods in the store can be obtained.

Supermarkets use new technology to make paying for goods quicker and easier.

Although we can order pizzas by telephone or have our newspapers or mail-order goods delivered to our home, people still love to go out shopping. There are a large number of ways to shop whether we go to a high street with lots of shops, a shopping centre, outdoor market or to a street stall. It is an enjoyable way to spend some of our free time. It is hard to imagine a time when we will never leave the house to shop, despite the invention of television shopping channels and home-computers.

Although new technology is used in many shops, you can still buy flowers from street stalls.

TIMELINE

5000 BC	4000 BC	690 BC	100 BC	AD 79
In the Middle East crops were grown.

People began bartering flint and metal for crops. | Trade routes set up in the Middle East and around the Mediterranean. | The first gold and silver coins were used instead of bartering. | The Romans began building towns with forums (central market places). | Pompeii, in Italy, buried in ash by the volcano Vesuvius. The shops and markets were preserved. |

8000s	10000s	1200s	1295	
Fairs became poular in China. The fairs were highly organized and regulated.	Trade began to increase in Europe and Asia.

Merchant guilds started in Europe. | Fairs became popular in Europe, as they had done in the ninth century. | Marco Polo returned from China to Venice, Italy. He wrote about the organized markets and shops in China. |  |

1300s	1600s		1700s	1847
Large markets such as Tenochtitlan, now in modern-day Mexico, grew up in the Aztec Empire.	Shops in Europe began to use small panes of glass in their windows.		Luxury goods such as silks, furs and glassware are traded from country to country.	First canned meat sent abroad from Australia to Britain.

1850s	1868	1877	1879	1884
Shops lit by gas lamps.

First department store opened in Paris, France. | Large-scale canning of meat began in Chicago, USA. | Refrigerated meat sent from Uruguay to France. | Frank Woolworth opened his first five-cent store in Pennsylvania, USA. | Marks and Spencer started a market stall in England which later became a chain of shops in many countries. |

1924	1949	1960		1970
Clarence Birdseye started a company to freeze food, which now sells food throughout the world.	Birdseye invented a process speeding up the freezing time for food.	Canada permitted the irradiation of potatoes.		Bar codes invented and introduced into packaging in many shops.

GLOSSARY

Archaelogical sites Land which has been dug up in order to study the past.

Aztecs The ancient people of Mexico between 1340 and 1500.

Bazaar A covered market area, particularly found in Eastern cities.

Brands Trade names given to goods being sold.

Catalogue Books describing goods which can be ordered by post.

Check-out The area where you pay at a supermarket.

Conquistadors The Spanish army which invaded Mexico in the sixteenth century.

Craftspeople People who are skilled at jobs using their hands. Crafts include weaving, carpentry and metalwork.

Dehydrated Food that has had the water removed from it in order to preserve it.

Drapery shop A shop that sells different kinds of materials for making clothes.

Escalators Moving staircases.

Flints Very hard stones that can be split and sharpened to make tools.

Guilds Associations of craftspeople who do similar work.

Imported Goods bought in from other countries.

Information technology (IT) Ways of using computers to send or receive information.

Infra-red scanner A machine which uses light to read bar codes on goods in shops.

Irradiation A way of making fruit and vegetables last longer. Low levels of radiation are passed through them.

Ivory The hard white material which forms the tusks of elephants. Ivory is very beautiful and in the past it was made into jewellery.

Jade A hard stone, usually green in colour, which is used for making ornaments.

Lathes Cutting machines used for making round objects.

Merchants Traders.

Middle East The countries at the eastern end of the Mediterranean Sea, including Saudi Arabia, Iraq and Iran.

Nitrogen A gas without any colour, taste or smell.

Plate glass Sheets of glass made in large pieces.

Porcelain A hard, white clay which is used to make plates and bowls.

Preserve Made to last longer. For example, food can be preserved by freezing.

Quality The standard of excellence of goods. Expensive goods are often called quality goods.

Spices Seeds or plants, such as nutmeg or pepper, used for flavouring food.

Taxes Money paid to the government in order to pay for public services.

Warehouse A building in which goods are stored before they are sold.

INDEX

Numbers in **bold** indicate subjects shown in pictures as well as in the text.

BOOKS TO READ

Shopping, by Gill Tanner and Tim Wood,
A & C Black 1994

Investigating Shopping, by Selma
Montford, Young Library Ltd 1993

Pompeii, by Peter Connolly, Oxford
University Press 1990

Finding Out About Packaging, Franklin
Watts 1990

The Shopkeeper, by Anne Stewart, Evans
1991

Shopping Centre, by Neil and Ting Morris,
Evans 1991

PLACES TO VISIT

The Ironbridge Gorge Museum
Telford
Shropshire, TF8 7AW, England

Markham District Historical Museum
9350 HiWay
Markham, ON L3P 3J3
Canada

The Rocks Heritage and Information Centre
George Street
Sydney, NSW 2000
Australia